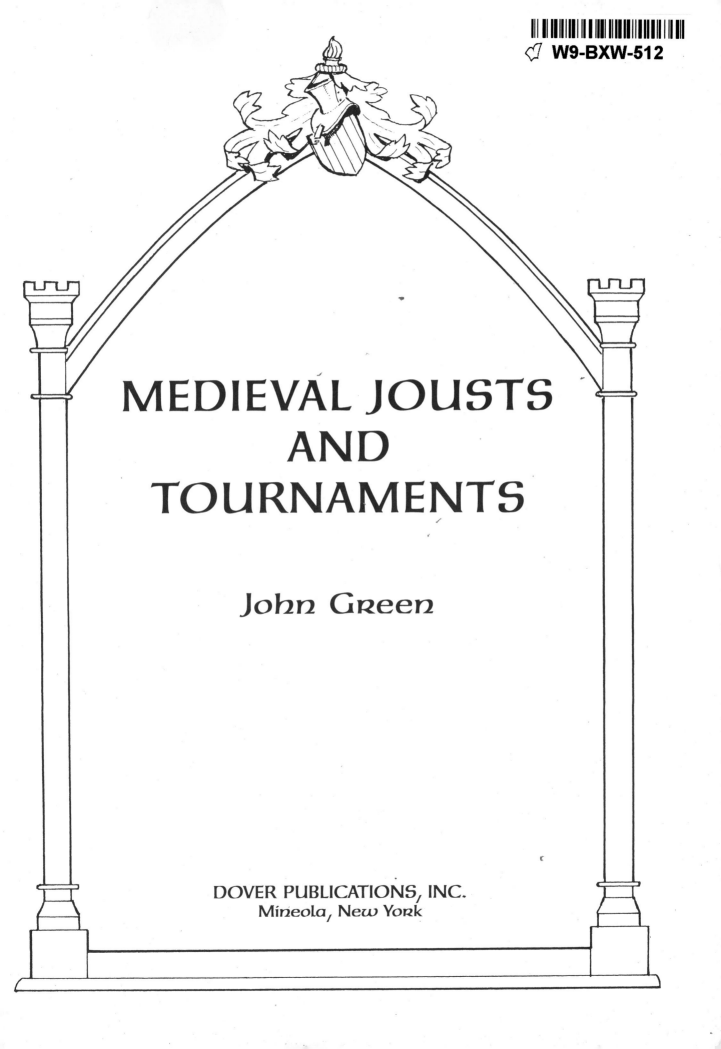

MEDIEVAL JOUSTS
AND
TOURNAMENTS

John Green

DOVER PUBLICATIONS, INC.
Mineola, New York

Copyright

Bibliographical Note

Medieval Jousts and Tournaments is a new work, first published by Dover Publications, Inc., in 1998.

DOVER *Pictorial Archive* SERIES

This book belongs to the Dover Pictorial Archive Series. You may use the designs and illustrations for graphics and crafts applications, free and without special permission, provided that you include no more than four in the same publication or project. (For permission for additional use, please write to Permissions Department, Dover Publications, Inc., 31 East 2nd Street, Mineola, N.Y. 11501.)

However, republication or reproduction of any illustration by any other graphic service, whether it be in a book or in any other design resource, is strictly prohibited.

International Standard Book Number
ISBN-13: 978-0-486-40135-5
ISBN-10: 0-486-40135-9

Manufactured in the United States of America
Dover Publications, Inc., 31 East 2nd Street, Mineola, N.Y. 11501

INTRODUCTION

Tournaments and jousts were an important part of life in the Middle Ages from the 11th century on. Like modern sports events, they attracted competitors, spectators, and honored guests from near and far. The stars of the war games were the knights, young men of the nobility who eagerly competed with each other at the risk of serious injury and even death.

The games originated among warriors in what historians call the Dark Ages, the five centuries after the disintegration of the Roman Empire in the year 500. To keep themselves in fighting shape, and as a way to bring some life to the periods of boredom between battles, knights challenged each other to mock combat. Generally on horseback and using lances and swords as weapons, the men engaged in fierce fights. Rules were few and informal, and injuries were frequent. The matches were generally held in the open countryside, sometimes wreaking havoc on a peasant's land.

The overlords to whom the knights had pledged military service grew concerned about the number of their young men who were injured in these games. Eventually, it was decided that the mock battles should be better organized and more closely regulated. Judges, referees, and other officials were appointed to control the contests. Nobles and even kings and queens began to play host to tournaments, which now took place near castles and towns and attracted invited guests and other spectators. Even so, many events still turned into brawls. In 1130 Pope Innocent II condemned the violence and threatened to excommunicate participants.

The feudal system began to decay in the 15th century, as new modes of warfare made knights less important in battle. At the same time tournaments held on to their popularity, often emphasizing color and pageantry over combat. Events became more formal, and sometimes the participants acted out plots that recalled some moment of past glory or paid homage to royalty. By the end of the 17th century, medieval tournaments had faded into history.

Medieval Hero. Knights in armor were a familiar sight in England and western Europe during the Age of Chivalry. Skilled in warfare and in horsemanship, knights were the foundation on which feudal society was built. They were sworn to protect both church and state and to uphold such chivalric virtues as Piety, Honor, Bravery, Sacrifice, and Loyalty. In return for military service to king or lord, knights were often granted a landed estate and a share in the spoils of war.

War games. When not fighting against their lord's enemies, knights often practiced for war at mock battles. These early tournaments began in France during the 11th century. The field of battle was an enclosure near a castle, as in the drawing, or in open country. The enclosed field came to be called *the lists* in England. In the main event, which was called a *mêlée*, two teams of mounted knights fought each other with swords and lances.

Training for knighthood. Boys of noble birth were often sent to an overlord's castle to learn the arts of battle and the rules of chivalry. They began as pages, then around the age of 14 became squires, apprenticed to knights. Here two youths engage in a mock duel while others practice jousting at the quintain, a post with a revolving cross-piece. Their objective is to hit the shield at one end with their lances and then quickly move to avoid being struck by the sandbag at the other end.

Fighting in a *mêlée*. On foot and on horseback, knights battle each other at close quarters. Two types of helmets are worn here—the flat-top great helm with eye-slits and ventilation holes and the older Norman-style headgear with nose guard. The knights' body armor, called mail, consists of thousands of metal rings joined together. Their shields are wooden and painted on each side. In spite of this protective gear, injuries and even deaths did occur in tournaments.

Last rites of the church. Religious faith was an important part of chivalry. Here a priest gives the sacrament of extreme unction to a knight who may die from injuries suffered in a tournament. Whether his body could be buried by the church was another matter. In 1130 Pope Innocent II condemned violent sport and declared that no one who died in a tournament could be buried in sanctified ground. Many priests did not honor the ban, which remained in effect until 1316.

Breaking both lances. The sharp crack of one of the big lances being broken in combat was sure to bring cheers from tournament spectators. Perhaps to please the crowds, jousters in the late Middle Ages used hollow lances rather than the stronger lances made for war. Breaking a lance was one of the ways to score points in a joust, as was landing a blow on an opponent. Hitting a rival's horse, on the other hand, was grounds for disqualification.

Unhorsing a rival. The joust became an important part of many tournaments. The primary goal was for a knight to manipulate his lance so as to knock an opponent to the ground. Here invited guests in the gallery and commonfolk on foot watch as a 12th-century champion, William Marshal, unseats another rival. Like many tournament competitiors, Marshal was also a hero in war, serving in the armies of Henry II and Richard the Lion-Hearted.

Holding a prisoner for ransom. As in war, some tournament competitors suffered the humiliation of being captured. It was accepted practice for the victors to seize their prisoners' horses and armor and to hold the men for ransom. Here, too, William Marshal was a champion. During one year he is said to have captured over 100 knights. Prisoners who were taken after suffering injuries were generally well cared for, according to the traditions of chivalry.

Knight-errant. A young knight and his squire pause before riding on to the tournament where he will face his first important competition. Young noblemen who were without land or other wealth often lived as knights-errant, roving the land in search of adventure and romance. In the combat offered by tournaments they found not only an outlet for their restless spirits but also the chance to gain honor, glory, and the booty captured by victorious knights.

12

Eager for combat. One of the most famous knights-errant was Ulrich von Lichtenstein, a German. Fighting off all challengers in defense of his honor and that of his lady, he was said to have broken over 300 lances in just one month of competition. To men like von Lichtenstein, knighthood was more a spiritual calling than a career. They lived and died by the rules of chivalry. The ornate crest on his helmet was worn for tournament events, not for wartime battles.

Climax of the joust. The intensity of the early jousts is portrayed in this scene. The knight on the left has been knocked off balance by his rival's lance, now embedded in his shield, and is being lifted off his horse. Even with their high, rigid saddle-backs, called cantles and seen here at the right, riders were not always able to remain on their mounts. Once driven to the ground, most knights found it difficult to move freely in their heavy armor. Squires stand by at the right ready to help,

if permitted, or to supply new lances. Over time, jousts became formalized, with rules that governed proper conduct and scoring. Knights who were unhorsed generally lost the match outright. In jousts in which there was no "knock-down," points were awarded for blows that hit home and for other actions that penetrated an opponent's defenses. The tents in the background were common sights at many large tournaments, where they were set up as headquarters for visiting nobles.

Ready for battle. A colorful part of tournament pageantry was the coats of arms and other devices of heraldry worn by the participants. Here a knight parades before the gallery holding his banner and shield, with ribands streaming from his helmet crest. The horse's coat is similarly decorated. Heraldry came into being in the 12th century as a way of identifying the competing knights, who otherwise looked alike in their helmets and body armor.

16

Grooming the knight's warhorse. Called a destrier, the horse ridden by the knight in tournament combat was bred to be aggressive, to bite and kick and otherwise attempt to injure opponents and their mounts. Destriers also had to be strong enough to carry a knight in armor for long periods. Other horses were used for general-purpose riding, and mules and donkeys carried the knight's baggage. The squire was responsible for the care of all these animals.

Delivering the challenge. A messenger from the tournament host proffers a blunted sword of arms at a formal ceremony of invitation. The lord's acceptance of the sword means that he and his entourage will participate in the competition. It is then his privilege to select the judges from a list submitted for approval. Less-formal invitations are sent to spectators and other participants, sometimes months in advance for major tournaments with many guests.

"The tournament is about to begin." Heralds announce the opening of a tournament. As these competitions became more popular, the importance of the heralds increased. Not only did they 'herald' the beginning of the games, but they also helped organize, judge, and score the events. Perhaps most significant, heralds became experts at identifying the competitors by their colors and crests, eventually giving such emblems the name by which they became known—heraldry.

Arrival at the tournament. Tournaments were great spectacles, a break in the gray tedium of medieval life. Here a knight, his lady, and their entourage ride through town on their way to the competition. He is wearing a sallet—a helmet common in the 15th century—and a tunic made of plate armor. The lady's colorful gown is topped by a flamboyant veiled hat called a hennip. The boy in the foreground raises his sword in salute to his hero, the knight in shining armor.

20

Ladies view the display. Many tournaments involved more than *mêlées* and jousts. They were elitist events, staged by and for the nobility, who were often eager to show off their emblems of rank and power. Before the main competition began, knights and their supporters displayed colors and banners, coats of arms and other heraldry, and helmets with elaborate crests. The ladies' hats, worn indoors and out, were typical of the period.

Vying for honor. Here, knights in armor and their horses in colorful regalia parade before a gallery of ladies who will choose the tournament's knight-of-honor. If a woman identified a man who had mistreated her in the past, he would be banned from taking part in the competition. In fact, any knight who was known to have behaved in an unchivalrous manner, perhaps by breaking a promise or by lending money for interest, would also be banned.

Opening the tournament. As the competitors wait to enter the lists, the knight-of-honor cuts the entrance rope. Tournament pageantry was described by the French poet Chrétien de Troyes in his 12th-century romance *Erec*: "Many a pennon flew there, vermilion, blue and white . . . many a lance was carried there, painted in silver and white, others in gold and blue, and many more of different kinds, some banded and some spotted . . . The field is completely covered with arms."

A lady gives her favor. As the young woman ties a favor, or token of her love, onto the knight's arm, he in turn vows to dedicate his performance in the tournament to her. Unusually for the time, her long tresses are uncovered by any hat or veil— perhaps an indication of her high regard for the handsome knight. Songs and stories of the day glorified courtly love, praising the selfless passion and pure adoration that was felt by knights for their ladies.

Dangerous swordplay. In the heat of a *mêlée* even a mock battle could turn violent. Here the combat is deadly serious even though the swords' sharp tips are blunted or covered. Knights held their weapons, especially swords, in high esteem, often having them blessed by a priest. Many swords were named, like King Arthur's Excalibur. The soldiers standing by here carry wooden staves to separate combatants who become dangerously entangled.

Knight in jousting armor. Both knight and horse in the foreground are ready for their turn at the joust. With the limited visibility provided by the frog-mouthed helmet, and with his hands full holding lance and shield, the knight will rely on the help of his well-trained horse to maneuver into strong positions during the joust. In the background, the combatants have broken each other's lances. The knight on the right is about to be forced off his horse.

Sacred occasion. At a church ceremony the page, typically age 14, is advanced to the rank of squire. The lad kneels to swear loyalty to his lord and to receive a sword and a belt. The squire will then begin his service as apprentice to a knight and learn at first hand the ways of war and the customs of chivalry. After the formal ceremony there was generally a celebration, accompanied by an exhibition of horsemanship and other skills by the new squire and others in the household.

The accolade. In the early Middle Ages, the ceremonies of chivalry were often performed in the field. Here a knight dubs his squire a knight with a gentle tap on the shoulder. (In other cases the sword was brought down with a resounding "thwack.") Some men were knighted before going into battle, others after displaying bravery and prowess in combat. In later times, the accolade, as the ceremonial tap was called, often took place in a church or royal palace.

Barriers to prevent injury. In the 15th century barriers called tilts were built to keep the jousting knights separate from each other. The primary purpose of the barriers was to prevent head-on collisions and subsequent injury to the knights and their horses. Here a combatant breaks his lance unseating an opponent. While the defeated knight disappointed his lady and embarrassed himself, he was not seriously hurt, and later returned to the fight.

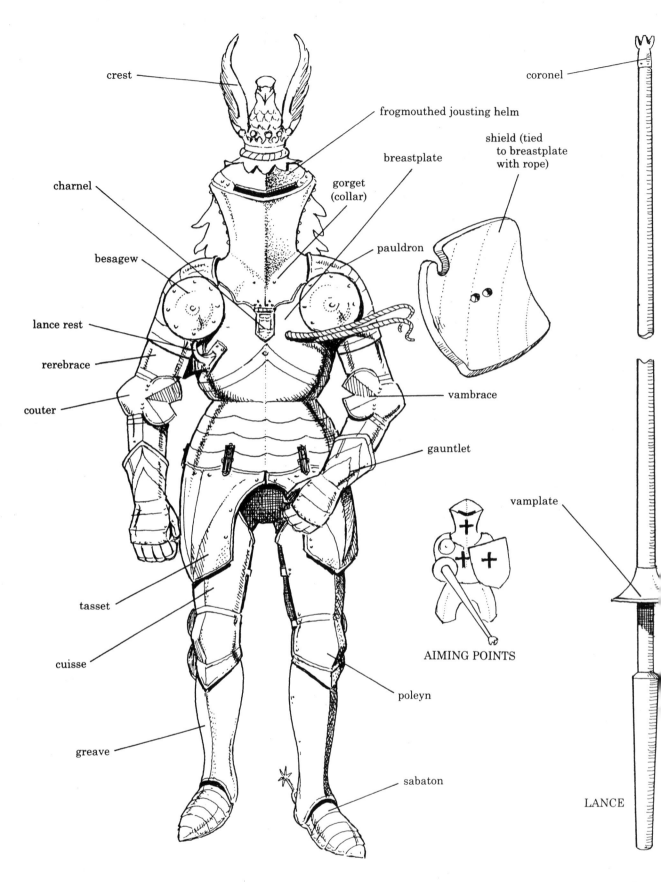

crest

frogmouthed jousting helm

breastplate

shield (tied to breastplate with rope)

charnel

gorget (collar)

pauldron

besagew

lance rest

rerebrace

couter

vambrace

gauntlet

vamplate

tasset

cuisse

poleyn

AIMING POINTS

greave

sabaton

coronel

LANCE

Knight and horse in armor. The important parts of a suit of armor typical of the 15th century are identified in these drawings. Over the 500 or so years when knights were the dominant force in most of the battles and wars in Europe, armor evolved from simple chain mail—interwoven metal rings that had protected soldiers since the days of the Roman imperial army—to the complex, cumbersome, but virtually impregnable metal suit illustrated here. Aiming points, marked with crosses,

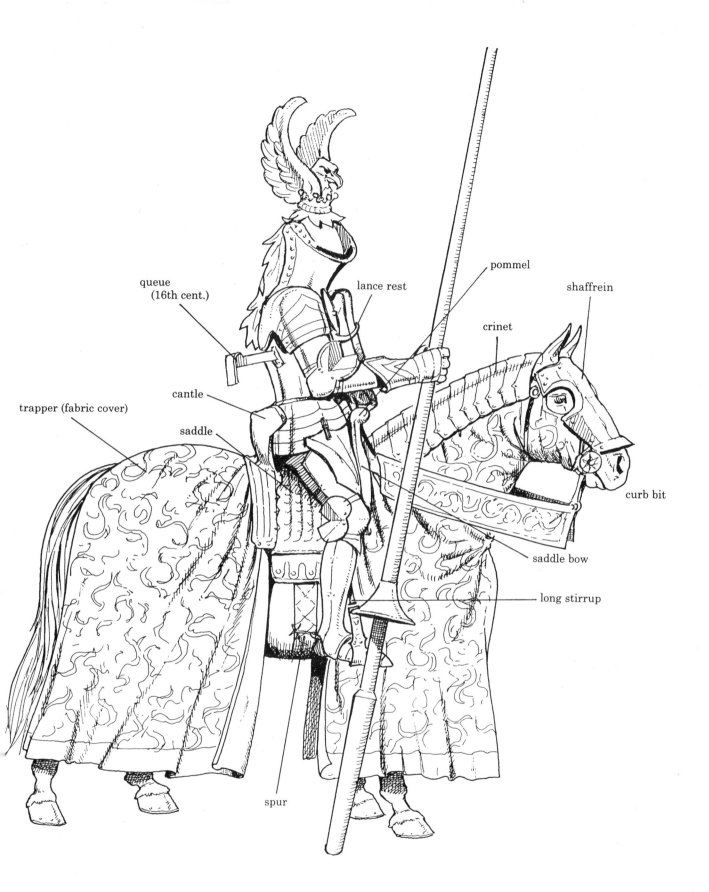

queue
(16th cent.)

lance rest

pommel

shaffrein

crinet

cantle

trapper (fabric cover)

saddle

curb bit

saddle bow

long stirrup

spur

are the primary targets for the opposing knight's lance, In most tournaments the lance's sharp tip was covered by a coronel, which was more likely to shatter lances and unhorse opponents than to inflict injury. As illustrated, horses were cloaked and armored almost as thoroughly as their riders. Unlike many medieval artifacts, armor has been preserved through the ages, so that today many fine examples of medieval battle dress can be seen in museums.

Jousting at Westminster Palace. Henry VIII was famous as a jouster, here breaking a lance as he unseats his opponent. He was also enthusiastic in supporting tournaments as a way of keeping his knights primed and ready for battle. In 1511, at the age of 20, Henry spent 4,000 English pounds—a king's ransom at the time—to stage a lavish tournament at his palace in London. On display today in the Tower of London is one of Henry's suits of armor, which weighs 93 pounds.

Blunted swords. A popular tournament event was one-on-one combat with swords blunted to prevent bloodshed. Mounted or on foot, knights tried to subdue their opponents with powerful blows that were only partly deflected by shields and armor.

Both knights are wearing cage-type helmets made for combat with mace or sword. The rider with upraised sword and his horse are both in armor emblazoned with the fleur-de-lis, a heraldic symbol associated with France.

Royal summit meeting. In 1520, Henry VIII met Francis I of France in a conference of "peace and friendship" near Calais, France. Temporary palaces were built for the two courts, and the splendor was such that the meeting-place came to be known as the Field of the Cloth of Gold. Part of the pageantry was a tournament in which the two kings and their armies competed in jousts and other events. Henry supplied his men with more than 3,000 lances.

34

Foot combat with poleaxes. Often, after jousting, knights fought each other on foot. Pole-axes (originally spelled pollaxes) were deadly weapons, but knights were protected by their armor. The steel hooped skirts, called tonlets, provided more mobility than standard leg armor. Contests on foot were generally won by the knight with the stamina to absorb blow after blow and outlast his opponent, who often collapsed from exhaustion.

Advancing at full tilt. Horse and rider present a fearsome sight as they lunge into combat. Both are carrying a great deal of dead weight. The knight's besagew, a circular plate over his right armpit, is almost as large as the shield he carries on his left side. The large semi-circular shields protecting the knight's stirrups on each side of the horse will help him to hold his seat despite attacks by his opponent trying to throw him off his mount.

Finishing a coat of mail. Master craftsman forges the final links in a tunic made of mail. Worn on the body over fabric or on the head under a helmet, this type of armor was made of interlocking metal rings. Mail dates from the Roman Empire and continued to be worn in Europe until at least the 14th century. Even after it was replaced by armor plate, especially for tournament wear, mail continued to be used when flexibility was important.

Armorers at work. Development of armor reached its peak in the 16th century. Custom-made suits were cut to shape from plates of iron or steel. Most knights wore their heaviest and most decorative armor in tournament competition, particularly the joust. The finest armor in Europe was produced in Germany and Italy, by workshops like this one at the court of Emperor Maximilian I. Pausing at the entrance to the shop are the emperor himself and a courtier.

Marshal of the lists. Primary responsibility for managing the tournament was given to the marshal of the lists. He enforced the regulations of the games and saw to it that the rules and customs of chivalry were followed. Along with judges, the marshal watched all the events and settled any disputes. To signal the end of combat, the marshal threw a white arrow in front of the contestants. Here the marshal of the lists wears his badge of office around his neck

Banquet at the castle. Since hospitality was an important part of medieval life, the noble host of a tournament provided at least one feast for his guests. Servants worked for days preparing such delicacies as the roast boar's head displayed by the serving-maid at the left. Meat pies, a variety of chickens and other fowl, cheese, and pastries were among other favorite foods. Imported spices were used generously in preparing the meal. Plates were of pewter, silver, or even gold. It

was considered proper to eat with one's fingers, though some people traveled with their own knives and other utensils. With large amounts of wine, beer, and other beverages on hand, the revels often continued through the night. Entertainers like the strolling flute player kept the guests diverted. There was also dancing, singing, and storytelling. Richly colored draperies and embroidered hangings warmed up the cold castle walls.

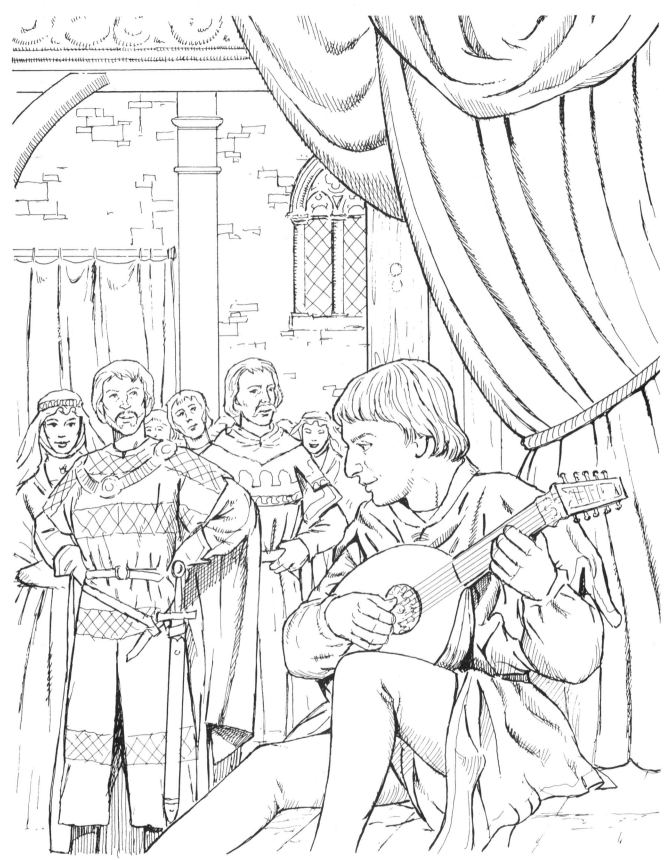

Songs and stories. Troubadors or, as they were sometimes called, minstrels were among the entertainers at banquets and other celebrations. Many were from southern France, and they traveled from place to place, singing of courtly love, the glory of battle, and other romantic subjects popular with the medieval nobility. Some of the troubadors' work, such as the *Song of Roland,* is still known today. In Germany these poet-musicians were called *minnesingers.*

Tournament fair. By the late Middle Ages, tournaments had become an opportunity for all classes of people to enjoy a holiday. They came from miles around to be part of the color and excitement. The nobles sometimes joined the common folk at open-air fairs near the tournament grounds. Trade, talk, and entertainment were in plentiful supply. The musician with the monkey on his shoulder is playing a medieval fiddle, forerunner of the modern violin.

Emperor Maxmilian I. The German ruler Maximilian I was a strong fighter with both lance and sword. Here he is shown in combat with one of his knights. As was the custom in Germany at the time, their swords' sharp tips are not blunted. Both men are wearing cloth tunics over their body armor, which is more flexible than the heavy suits worn by knights on horseback. The leg armor is designed for easier movement on foot.

Death of a king. Royalty took part in many tournaments but seldom suffered serious injury. An exception was Henri II of France, who died in 1559 at the age of 40. In Paris to celebrate his daughter's wedding, he jousted with his friend Gabriel, comte de Montgomery. After the men shattered each other's lances, Montgomery failed to lower his broken lance quickly enough, and it smashed into Henri's face. A splinter entered the king's visor and pierced his temple, killing him.

Honoring Queen Elizabeth I. Tournaments continued as ceremonial occasions until the beginning of the 17th century. In London from about 1580 on, tournaments were held almost every year to celebrate the accession to the throne of Queen Elizabeth I. These tournaments were more about pageantry and theatricality than displaying the martial skills of individual knights. Some events were nonviolent, choreographed representations of the knights' love for their queen.

Mechanical target. By the 16th century most tournaments had evolved from tests of battle skills to performances designed as entertainment for spectators. Clothing, armor, and weapons were elaborately decorated, and technology grew more important, especially in Germany. In the *mechanisches rennen,* the mechanical joust, a segmented piece of armor was designed with a hidden spring that caused it split apart when it was hit squarely by a lance.

Awards ceremony. Just as a knight-of-honor was chosen to open a tournament, so a queen of beauty was chosen to present the prizes at the end of the competition. The awards were not of great value, being small gemstones or trinkets made of gold or silver, but they had importance as tokens of a knight's skill and courage. The real prizes for the winners were the armor, weapons, and especially the horses they took from those whom they defeated in combat.